94'

D I S C O V E R
Rocks&Minerals

Contributing writer:
Dr. Joel E. Arem

Publications International, Ltd.

Consultant:
W.R.C. Shedenhelm

Louis Weber, C.E.O.
Publications International, Ltd.
7373 North Cicero Avenue
Lincolnwood, Illinois 60646

ISBN Number:
1-56173-107-2

Photo credits:

Front cover: Joel E. Arem
Back cover: Bob Jones

Joel E. Arem: Front cover, front endsheet, title page, table of contents,
6–12, 14–17, 19–25, 27–29, 30–43, back endsheet; **D. Dietrich/FPG:**
19; **Bob Jones:** Front endsheet, title page, table of contents, 4–6, 10,
11, 21, 24, 27, 28, 30–32, 34–38, 40, 43, back endsheet, back cover;
Cheryl Kemp/Photo-Nats: 14; **W. Kina/FPG:** 18; **Lee Kuhn/
FPG:** 18; **John Michael/International Stock:** 25; **Jeffrey Scovil:** 9;
George Schwartz/FPG: 16; **Stan Sholik/FPG:** 41; **R. Smith/FPG:** 17;
David Stone/Photo-Nats: 8; **Bob Taylor/FPG:** 18; **Herb Thomas/
FPG:** 12; **Ron Thomas/FPG:** 12, 13; **Kim Todd/Photo-Nats:** 20;
Zeismann/FPG: 42.

Illustrations: Pablo Montes O'Neill; Lorie Robare

Dr. Joel E. Arem
Contributing writer

Contributing writer Dr. Joel E. Arem holds a Ph.D. in mineralogy
from Harvard University. He served as the director of the geology
program at the Brooklyn Children's Museum and is widely published
in the field of rocks, minerals, and gems. His two children provided
invaluable support and perspective in writing this manuscript.

W.R.C. Shedenhelm
Consultant

Consultant W.R.C. Shedenhelm has been the senior editor of
Rock & Gem magazine for close to 20 years. He teaches
geology and mineralogy and is the author of several books
on rocks for young people.

CONTENTS

WHAT ARE MINERALS?

They are the building blocks of the earth, moon, and planets. We use some minerals, such as gold and silver, as money. We write with other minerals. The "lead" in a pencil is the mineral graphite. We even eat minerals. Table salt is the mineral halite!

But what are minerals made of? Atoms make up rocks and minerals. Atoms are so small that millions can fit inside a period. There are about 100 different kinds of atoms. They often attach to each other in groups called molecules. Our air is made of atoms and molecules.

The atoms and molecules inside the earth move around and bump into each other. Sometimes they stick together in rows and layers that are smooth and even. The layers can build up to form mineral crystals. These can be very beautiful and valuable.

4

MINERAL PROPERTIES

We use special words to describe minerals. These words, called properties, tell about the way minerals look and the way they stick together.

If iron gets into beryl, it will be yellow or blue. A bit of manganese makes it pink. Chromium turns beryl green. These colored crystals are pretty and beryl is often cut into gemstones.

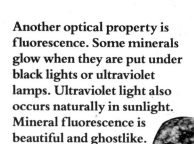

Another optical property is fluorescence. Some minerals glow when they are put under black lights or ultraviolet lamps. Ultraviolet light also occurs naturally in sunlight. Mineral fluorescence is beautiful and ghostlike.

Optical Properties

Optical properties tell us what happens to light going through a mineral. One optical property is color. Minerals have some of the strongest and richest colors you will ever see. Vermeer, a famous painter, used a special blue paint that is named after him (Vermeer blue). His secret ingredient was lazurite. The color of some minerals is caused by the atoms that make them. Copper minerals are mostly blue and green. Manganese minerals are usually pink.

Some minerals have no color at all. Sometimes nearby atoms get inside the growing crystal. This can change colorless minerals into different colors. The atoms that do not belong are called impurities.

Luster is the optical property that explains the way a mineral reflects light. All minerals are either metallic (they look like metals) or non-metallic (they don't).

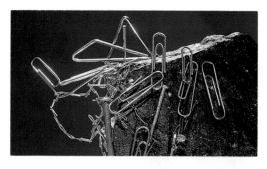

Bulk Properties

The most important bulk property is density. Density is how much a mineral weighs compared to water. Another bulk property is magnetism. Lodestone attracts small bits of iron, such as paper clips.

Mechanical Properties

The mechanical properties of crystals are caused by atoms sticking together in different ways. There are minerals that have different properties even though they are made of the same atoms.

Hardness is a very important mechanical property. The hardness of a mineral is determined by how easily it can be scratched if rubbed against another mineral.

A long time ago, a scientist named Friedrich Mohs put minerals in the order of which one would scratch the others. Mohs created a number scale, called the Mohs Hardness Scale, using ten common minerals. Number 10 is the hardest, and one is the softest.

On the Mohs Scale your fingernail is about a two and a copper penny is a three.

THE MOHS HARDNESS SCALE

1. Talc	6. Feldspar
2. Gypsum	7. Quartz
3. Calcite	8. Topaz
4. Fluorite	9. Corundum
5. Apatite	10. Diamond

Cleavage is the mechanical property of minerals that describes how it breaks. If a mineral breaks unevenly, the break is called fracture. But if a mineral breaks only in certain directions, it has cleavage.

Mineral properties happen because minerals are built of rows of atoms.

A good example of cleavage is the mineral mica. This mineral has perfect cleavage. Mica can be split into paper-thin layers with a knife blade. The mineral above shows fracture.

HOW CRYSTALS GROW

Crystals are made of layers of neatly stacked atoms. A crystal starts with a tiny "seed." The crystal gets bigger and bigger as the right atoms are added to the seed.

These crystals were grown in a solution.

Atoms must be able to move to just the right place in order to fit into a crystal. Atoms floating around in a liquid or a gas can move. They move over the surface of a growing crystal until they find the right place to stick. Once an atom is in place, it can vibrate a bit, but it can't move.

Mineral crystals sometimes grow in gases, like the ones found coming out of volcanoes. Most crystals grow in liquids. The liquid can be a solution, which is hot water that has atoms floating in it. The liquid can also be a melt, like the melted rock magma that is found deep within the earth.

Minerals from a Melt

The inside of the earth is very hot. Most rocks stay melted until they get near the surface. When melted rock (magma) cools, the atoms start to form crystals. A melted rock usually has many different kinds of atoms in it. These atoms can form many different kinds of crystals.

Magma reaching the surface and flowing out of a volcano is called lava, which forms rocks.

Minerals that grow in melted rock almost never become perfect crystals, because the crystals bump into each other. When the rock cools, different kinds of crystals are all jumbled together. This mixture is usually hard to see with just your eye.

Minerals Formed in Water

If magma gets close enough to the earth's surface it may find a crack in the rock. The water inside the magma can then fill the crack. This water is very hot and can contain an amazing number of different kinds of atoms. As the water cools (it can take thousands of years), the atoms start to form mineral crystals. Water is much thinner than melted rock, so the atoms can move around easily. Also, the crack in the rock is usually big enough so that the growing crystals don't bump into each other.

You can see the small crystals in a rock with a special kind of microscope. To do this you have to slice off a very thin piece of rock. Under the microscope you can see all the different crystals in the rock and how they grew together.

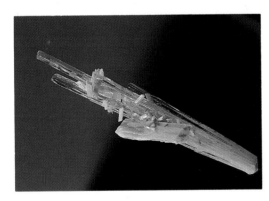

Mineral crystals that form this way are some of the most beautiful natural objects. These are the crystals that people travel miles to see in museums. Sometimes they look like flowers. The nicest of these crystals are sometimes clear enough for light to go through. These crystals may be cut as gemstones.

Sometimes crystals look like a bouquet of flowers.

9

MINERAL SHAPES

Atoms in crystals make special patterns. Each different mineral is made of different kinds of atoms.

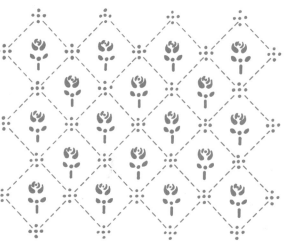

A good example of symmetry on a flat surface is wallpaper. Most wallpapers have repeating shapes that you see over and over as you look in different places.

The combination of a special pattern and special mixture of atoms is what makes each mineral different from every other mineral. Scientists have described more than 3,700 different minerals. The list grows every year as scientists find new ones.

The patterns in crystals are simple groups of shapes. These shapes are described by the way they look if you turn them around and around in different directions. The way a shape looks when you turn it all around is called symmetry.

A crystal doesn't have pictures on it, but it does have flat areas called crystal faces. Symmetry in a crystal means that if you turn the crystal around and around you see faces with the same shape over again. The symmetry in the crystal is described by the number of times the same face appears.

A cube (the shape of your first toy: the alphabet block!) has four-fold symmetry. All the faces on the cube are squares. If you hold the cube between your fingers and turn it completely around one time you see a square four times. Other shapes may have faces that appear twice (two-fold symmetry) or even six times (six-fold symmetry).

Along with being different colors, beryl often forms different crystal shapes.

10

Mineral shapes can be very complicated. Some crystals have more than 100 different faces! People who studied minerals in the last century spent most of their time describing crystals and drawing pictures of them.

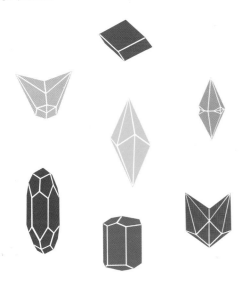

Perhaps the most fascinating thing about minerals is that a single mineral can form a hundred different-shaped crystals! Calcite forms all the shapes on the left. On the right and below, topaz also forms many shapes.

How Big Do Minerals Grow?

A mineral crystal will grow as long as there is space around it and atoms to attach to it. The crystals that grow in hot water inside cracks can be very large. You can see crystals in museums that are as tall as a person.

Crystals of the mineral spodumene from the Etta Mine in South Dakota were nearly 40 feet long. Giant crystals of quartz from Brazil weighed more than 10 tons (about the same as six cars). A crystal of feldspar discovered in Russia was reported to be as big as two railroad boxcars. But perhaps the largest of all is a crystal of beryl found in Madagascar in 1976. It was 59 feet long, almost 12 feet across, and weighed 187 tons!

Giant crystals of gypsum were found in Mexico. The crystals are so large that the place they came from is known as the Cave of Swords.

These large crystals are from a cave in Mexico.

11

WHAT ARE ROCKS?

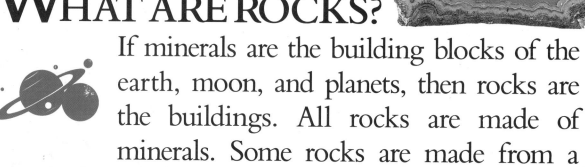

If minerals are the building blocks of the earth, moon, and planets, then rocks are the buildings. All rocks are made of minerals. Some rocks are made from a single mineral. Other rocks are made of several minerals. Geology is the science of studying rocks to understand the history of earth.

Rocks form the beautiful mountains all over planet earth. The Grand Canyon is a geology lesson on how rocks formed. The sand on beaches was once large rocks—but the pounding of water and changes in weather broke the rocks into sand.

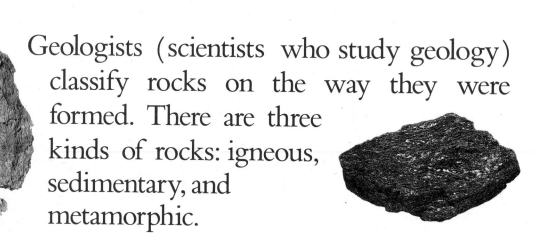

Geologists (scientists who study geology) classify rocks on the way they were formed. There are three kinds of rocks: igneous, sedimentary, and metamorphic.

IGNEOUS ROCKS

Igneous rocks are created when magma (melted rock within the earth) cools.

If lava cools inside the earth, the igneous rock is called intrusive. If lava cools on the earth's surface, the rock that forms is called extrusive. Extrusive rocks are the result of volcanic eruptions—when magma spills out of cracks or explodes into the air! Magma that reaches the surface in this way is called lava.

A dike is an intrusive formation that cuts across rock layers. Dikes are very easy to see because they are usually a different color from the rocks they cut across.

Intrusive Rocks

Intrusive rocks form large masses within the earth. The largest of these is called a batholith, and some batholiths are as large as 100,000 square miles. A batholith usually increases in size going downward. The melted rock at the top of a batholith might push up to form a volcano.

A laccolith is an intrusive rock formation that forces its way between layers of rock and usually pushes them up into a dome shape. Sometimes the bottom and top of the laccolith are flat. This kind is known as a sill.

The Grand Tetons are made of batholithic rock.

An igneous rock called a pegmatite has a coarse texture, which means the crystals in the rock are large. Pegmatites usually form underground but close to the earth's surface. Often they fill up large cracks so crystals may reach a very large size, sometimes many feet long. Pegmatites are usually made of three minerals: quartz, mica, and one of the members of the feldspar group.

Pegmatites are also special rocks because they may contain rare minerals— sometimes even gem minerals.

Granite is made of the same minerals as pegmatite, but the crystals in the rock are smaller. Granites are the main rock of batholiths, and are found all over the world. There are many different kinds of granite, depending on what minerals are present along with quartz and feldspar. Syenite is a rock that is like granite, but has no quartz and the crystals in it are smaller.

There are also dark colored intrusive rocks that usually form dikes and sills. Some of these rocks are called gabbro, diorite, monzonite, norite, and diabase. Finally, there is a group of intrusive rocks that are very dark colored and are made up of the minerals olivine and pyroxene. This group includes peridotite, dunite, and kimberlite.

Peridotite is made of the minerals olivine and pyroxene.

Kimberlite is rare but important. It is the rock in which diamonds are found!

15

IGNEOUS ROCKS

Extrusive Rocks

A volcano is an extrusive igneous formation. Volcanoes are made of lava. Lava is melted rock that has oozed out of cracks or exploded into the air and fallen back down in a cone-shaped pile.

Some volcanoes are formed under the sea. The lava bubbles out, makes clouds of steam, and then cools very quickly. The state of Hawaii is a group of islands in the Pacific Ocean. These islands are the tops of volcanoes that formed on the sea floor and grew in size until they poked out of the ocean. Some of the biggest mountains in the world are volcanoes. There are volcanos in South America that are nearly 23,000 feet tall.

Special rocks, called pyroclastic rocks, are made of pieces of melted rock that were thrown out of volcanoes, cooled in the air, and fell on the ground. Large pieces are called blocks. Smaller ones (less than an inch in size) are called cinders. A rock made up entirely of cinders is called scoria. Very fine volcanic powder is called ash. A rock made only of ash that has been squeezed and cemented together is called tuff.

Tuff (far left) is ash that has been cemented. Scoria (left) is rock made of cinders.

A volcano can be a small hill, or a mountain thousands of feet high. Mt. Ranier, in Washington, is a volcano.

A volcanic bomb is a blob of lava thrown into the air that cools in the shape of a giant teardrop.

Volcanoes are powerful and dangerous. The eruption of Mount Vesuvius in Italy in the year 79 A.D. buried the cities of Pompeii and Herculaneum in hot mud.

There are many interesting extrusive rocks. They are different from intrusive rocks mainly in their textures. The minerals in intrusive rocks could grow into crystals large enough to see with the eye. But the crystals in extrusive rocks did not have time to grow large. Most extrusive rocks have textures of crystals so small you need a magnifying glass to see them. Extrusive rocks are made of the same minerals as some intrusive rocks.

An unusual extrusive rock called porphyry contains different grain sizes. Porphyry started cooling within the earth, and large crystals had a chance to form. But then the rock was pushed out in a volcanic eruption. The part of the rock that was still melted cooled very quickly.

The most common extrusive igneous rock is basalt. This rock usually forms when lava cools. Basalt is dark, fine grained, and very tough. It is used all over the world for making roads. Basalt covers hundreds of thousands of square miles of the earth's surface. When the earth was very young, basalt was probably the most common rock.

Lava cools in different ways. Lava that cools with a jagged and rough surface is called aa (pronounced "ah-ah"). Lava that cools with a smooth, ropy surface is called pahoehoe (pronounced "pah-hoi-hoi").

THE ROCK CYCLE

Have you ever been to an ocean beach? Perhaps you have tried swimming in the surf and been knocked down by a big wave. Then you know about the power of water.

Rocks at the earth's surface are damaged by wind, rain, ice, and tiny animals and plants. Some of the gases in the air make an acid when they mix with rainwater. This acid can, over a long time, dissolve some kinds of rocks. Tiny plants called lichens also make acids that slowly wear away the rocks on which they live.

One interesting thing that results from the acid in falling rainwater is that some underground cracks in rocks are widened. The cracks become tunnels, and finally caverns.

Moving water can smash rocks hard enough to break them. After many years, the rocks are broken into sand. Look at beach sand with a magnifying glass. You will discover that it is a mixture of tiny bits of many different minerals. The name for the breaking up and wearing away of rocks at the earth's surface is weathering.

At one time, all the rocks on the earth's surface were igneous. The world was covered with volcanoes, and there were no oceans. But magma has water dissolved in it. After millions of years, the erupting volcanoes put enough water into the air to form clouds, and finally rain. Millions of years later enough rain had fallen to start making oceans.

Sometimes caves dry out. Water can drip from the ceiling and evaporate. This water has minerals in it, usually calcite. When the water disappears, it leaves interesting shapes. Long needles of rock may hang down from the ceiling—these are called stalactites. Needles that grow up from the floor are called stalagmites.

Without volcanic eruptions, the earth might not have its oceans.

Erosion is the name for all the ways that earth materials are moved around on the surface by wind and water.

The oceans and the rain started to wear away the igneous rocks over the earth's surface. Rain on the land turned into streams, and the streams into rivers. Moving water picked up the rock powder and dug into the land, carving holes and channels. In some places, the water filled up valleys and made lakes.

Every storm carried more rock pieces, large and small, into the waters. The layers got thicker and thicker. They got so thick that their weight squeezed all the water out of the sediments at the bottom of the pile. These sediments were pressed together so tightly that they became rocks. Rocks made in this way are called sedimentary rocks.

Movements of the earth pushed some of these sedimentary rocks up to the earth's surface. Water and wind treated these new rocks in the same way as the igneous rocks. The sedimentary rocks were torn apart and pushed into the streams, rivers, and oceans to make new sediments. Earth movements also pushed and squeezed both igneous and sedimentary rocks. The squeezing was so strong that the rocks were folded and bent. Sometimes this happened deep underground where it is very hot. Then the rocks were squeezed, folded, and also partly melted. Sometimes the minerals in the rocks were destroyed and new minerals were created.

Rocks formed by pressing, squeezing, and folding of other rocks are called metamorphic rocks.

The bits of rock, called sediments, carried by streams into lakes and oceans started to build up into thick layers.

19

SEDIMENTARY ROCKS

Most of the rocks we see at the earth's surface are sedimentary.

What makes sedimentary rocks different from other rocks is that they are usually layered.

Mechanical Sedimentary Rocks

Mechanical sedimentary rocks are made by a lake, stream bed, or ocean filling up with pieces of rocks that have been worn away by weathering.

Mechanical sedimentary rocks are usually cemented together. Nature's cement is the small amount of minerals dissolved in water. Imagine a thick pile of sand, pebbles, and clay buried deep underground. Water trickles through this pile and leaves tiny bits of minerals in the spaces between the sediments.

Another way of making a sedimentary rock is by squeezing. Clay pieces are small and flat. When these are piled in layers and squeezed, the water is squeezed out. The clay sheets stick together and form rock.

Rocks made of mineral bits that have been moved by water and settled into layers are called clastic rocks. Conglomerate is a cemented clastic rock made of large, rounded pieces.

The cement in a sandstone is often mixed with minerals that contain iron. These minerals are usually orange, red, yellow, or brown in color. The "painted deserts" in the western United States owe their bright colors to iron minerals.

Rocks made of clay are called shale and mudstone. The sediments in them are too small to see with a magnifying glass.

When smaller, sand-size grains are cemented together, the rock is called sandstone.

Arkose is an orangy-brown sandstone made of quartz and feldspar. Graywacke is a gray sandstone made of rock bits and clay.

Chemical Sedimentary Rocks

The most common minerals formed in sea water are calcite and dolomite. A rock made only of calcite is limestone.

The most common minerals formed in sea water are calcite and dolomite.

Some animals, such as clams, snails, and coral polyps, in the sea make shells out of minerals. These animals take carbon and oxygen out of sea water and make carbonate minerals in their bodies. Coquina is a limestone made of shells.

Coal is a sedimentary rock made of the remains of plants that lived in swamps millions of years ago. The plants died, fell into the swamp water, and were buried. The weight of the sediments pressed the ones at the bottom so tightly that they hardened into coal.

Evaporites are sedimentary rocks formed when surface water evaporates and minerals are left behind. The most important evaporite rocks are made of minerals halite and gypsum.

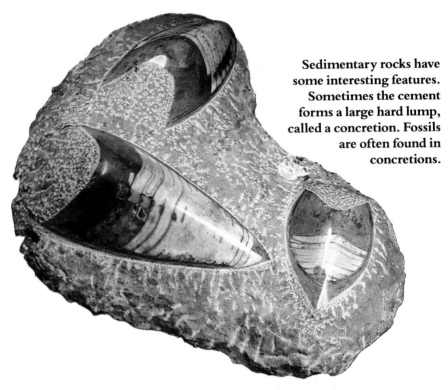

Sedimentary rocks have some interesting features. Sometimes the cement forms a large hard lump, called a concretion. Fossils are often found in concretions.

Sedimentary Features

Rounded lumps of mineral that are found inside other rocks are called nodules. Some nodules are made of very small crystals of quartz. The quartz can be stained by impurities. A nodule that forms with bands of color is agate. In jasper, the colors may form pictures.

Another sedimentary feature is bedding. You can see the different colors of rock and different grain sizes in those layers. This is what makes the Grand Canyon so amazing!

METAMORPHIC ROCKS

At the contact, a whole group of new minerals may be created. Minerals already present in both the igneous rock and the limestone are broken apart and reassembled into new minerals. This new rock is called a skarn.

Metamorphism means change of form. Metamorphic rocks are created by heat and pressure within the earth. Older rocks may be melted and squeezed and take on new forms.

Metamorphism is like baking a cake. If you put flour, eggs, milk, and sugar into a bowl and stir, you have batter. But if you put this into a pan and bake it, you have cake.

Metamorphic rocks have their own special appearance, or texture, as a result of squeezing. The most obvious one is layering, but not the same kind as we find in sediments. Metamorphic layering happens when the mineral crystals are squeezed until they are flattened. Sometimes the entire rock is folded and bent. Long, skinny mineral crystals may line up because of pressure.

Some metamorphic rocks are banded. The bands are caused by the minerals in the rock forming layers. Some metamorphic rocks also develop cleavage. This is not the same as the perfect cleavage in a mineral. Cleavage in a rock is a splitting in layers caused by the lining-up of flattened mineral crystals.

Regional metamorphism is a process that affects a large area, sometimes hundreds or thousands of square miles. Contact metamorphism happens when a hot igneous rock is forced into sedimentary rocks, such as limestone. The heat of the igneous rock causes many changes in the limestone. Most of these changes take place right where the igneous rock is touching the limestone (called the contact). The changes get less obvious farther inside the limestone.

Contact metamorphism is the effect of heat, pressure, and chemical changes in a small area, sometimes only as big as your bedroom.

22

We can list metamorphic rocks by describing the rocks they originally were. For example, if a shale is metamorphosed, it turns into the rock called slate.

Stronger metamorphism will turn the shale into a rock called phyllite. Phyllite has larger crystals than slate. These give the rock a shiny appearance.

Even stronger metamorphism will turn shales and other rocks into schist. Schist breaks with a kind of wavy surface. The rock looks twisted and bent because of the heat and pressure it has suffered. Different kinds of schist get their names from the kinds of minerals they contain.

Metamorphosed limestone is marble. Marble usually has a lovely pattern of dark swirls on a light gray or pink background. The dark pattern is made of minerals formed by heat and pressure from clays and other small mineral grains in the limestone. Marble is used all over the world for buildings, carvings, even furniture.

Igneous rocks can be metamorphosed also. Granite turns into a rock called gneiss (this word is pronounced "nice"). The minerals in a gneiss are the same as in granite, but the pressure of metamorphism has pushed them into layers.

This ruin marble is from Florence, Italy.

There are different kinds of gneiss. Like schist, gneiss is named by the minerals it contains.

STARTING YOUR COLLECTION

of rocks and minerals can begin today. Both rocks and minerals can be found almost anywhere. Sometimes  people find them in unexpected places— even in large cities. No matter where you live, there are rocks all around you.

Once you have started your collection, taking care of it is very important. You must learn how to organize and protect your rocks and minerals so that they last.

Rocks and minerals can tell you much about the earth and its history. Collecting rocks and minerals teaches you to care about the planet we live on.

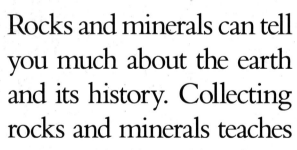

PROTECTING YOUR COLLECTION

Every major city has mineral and gem clubs. These clubs often have activities for young collectors.

Here is what you need to start collecting rocks and minerals:

1. A strong bag to hold what you find—a shoulder bag is best;
2. A hammer (special ones are made for breaking rocks);
3. Tissues, newspaper, or envelopes to wrap what you find;
4. A small notebook to record where and when you found each rock and to describe the surrounding area;
5. A magnifying glass;
6. Adhesive tape for putting numbers on each rock; and
7. Heavy gloves and safety glasses.

Storing Your Collection

Most rocks and minerals are hard, but not all. Hard minerals scratch softer ones. So, store minerals in a way that separates them. Some people use egg cartons.

Label everything. Paint a small spot on all your specimens with nail polish or white paint. Then label them with numbers. Using a small card, put the rock or mineral name, when you got it and where, and the collection number you wrote on the specimen.

Delicate specimens need special care. Cotton and tissues will protect them from bumping into each other. Some minerals darken in air or sunlight and should be stored in closed boxes. Others break apart if left in moist air. Small plastic bags will protect them.

ORGANIZING YOUR COLLECTION

Rocks are easy to collect and store. There are only three major rock types. Without special tools it is difficult to identify more than a small number of different rocks.

It is also difficult to decide how to organize a mineral collection— there are many different ways. You can arrange your minerals by color, or by crystal shape. Another way is to put all the minerals from one place together. You can even arrange everything alphabetically.

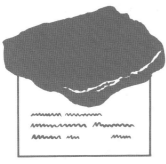

Scientists, museums, and serious collectors use a different system. This system was worked out by James D. Dana early in the 19th century. It arranges minerals by chemistry. A mineral collection that is carefully identified, labeled, and arranged by chemistry is called a systematic collection.

Some minerals are so common that you can find them almost anywhere. Others only come from one place on earth. Some minerals are so rare that the whole world supply would fit into a small bottle.

There are about 200 minerals prized by all serious collectors. This is because they are brightly colored, form shiny crystals, and are found in many different places.

Some collectors only collect the different habits of a single mineral.

Minerals may appear in many different shapes. The exact shape—called the habit—of a crystal depends on how it formed, and the impurities that were present when the crystal grew.

ELEMENTS

About 20 elements are found in pure form as minerals— these are called native elements. They are divided into the metals and the nonmetals.

Sulfur is yellow and brittle, and it is one of the nonmetals. Large sulfur crystals are found in Sicily, near Italy. Sulfur also comes out of volcanoes in the form of bad-smelling gases.

Silver nuggets almost always have some copper mixed into them. Silver also forms other interesting shapes. Some look like old trees.

Pure carbon is found in nature as two minerals: graphite and diamond. Graphite is the "lead" in pencils, but has many other uses. Diamond is a very valuable gemstone. Carbon is a nonmetal.

Copper is a much more common metal than silver or gold. There are many copper minerals.

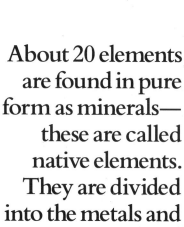

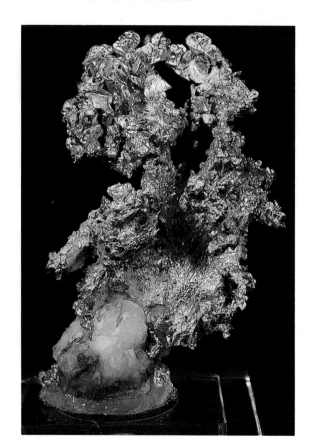

Gold nuggets may be very large and pure. Gold almost never forms compounds, but seems always to be found as native metal. Gold is also one of the heaviest metals.

SULFIDES

Galena is the most important ore of the metal lead. Lead has been used for centuries to make tubing, fishing sinkers, and bullets. It is a heavy metal, heavier than silver. Galena forms bright, silvery crystals that are usually shaped like cubes. These crystals are found in many places in the world.

Sphalerite is the main ore of the element zinc, which is another useful metal. Zinc is used in dry-cell batteries, paint, and in the chemical industry. Sphalerite is usually orange, red, brown, yellow, or green. Crystals are common throughout the world.

Cinnabar is the only important ore of the element mercury. Mercury is an unusual metal. It is very heavy, and is a liquid at room temperature. Cinnabar crystals are bright red. The best ones come from a mine in China.

Sulfides are compounds that have atoms of sulfur and atoms of a metal. The sulfides are important because they provide important metals. Minerals that are mined for their metals are called ores.

Marcasite is iron sulfide. It is brassy yellow and very common in all parts of the world. Iron sulfide also forms crystals where the iron and sulfur atoms are arranged differently than in marcasite. This other arrangement produces the mineral called pyrite. Pyrite is the most common sulfide mineral on earth and is found just about everywhere. Pyrite has many habits. Pyrite is brassy yellow and looks like gold. Pieces in streams have fooled miners, so it was nicknamed "fool's gold."

SULFOSALTS/HALIDES

Pyrargyrite, like proustite, is a sulfide of arsenic and silver. It is also red but is darker than proustite. The crystals are not as clear.

Halite is an evaporite mineral. It is found in thick layers that form when sea water evaporates. Sometimes it makes perfect cube-shaped crystals. These can be very large. Halite must be purified to make the table salt that we eat. But ground-up halite is put on roads to melt snow.

Sulfosalts are minerals that have sulfur, a metal (either silver, copper, or lead), and a semimetal. The semimetals are bismuth, antimony, and arsenic.

Proustite is the sulfosalt best known to collectors. It is also one of the prettiest of all minerals. Proustite is bright red. It is sometimes called "ruby silver." Crystals are bright, shiny, and sometimes clear.

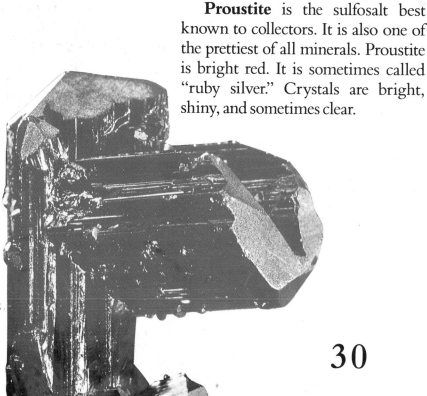

Fluorite is a compound of the metal calcium and the halogen gas fluorine. Fluorite makes cube-shaped crystals. These are found in many parts of the world, and can be many different colors. Fluorite is very beautiful and mineral collectors always want it in their collection.

OXIDES

Spinel is an oxide of magnesium and aluminum. It forms perfect crystals that can be many colors. Spinel is very hard and is often cut and polished as a gem. Other minerals that are similar to spinel are magnetite (an oxide of iron), and chromite (the oxide of the element chromium).

Bauxite is the only ore of the metal aluminum. Actually, bauxite should be called a rock because it is a mixture of several aluminum hydroxides.

The oxides are very important minerals. Oxygen is a part of the air we breathe. It is also in sea water, fresh water, and in magmas.

Hematite is iron oxide. The mineral is dark red, but always looks black unless it is broken into very small pieces. Hematite is found in many different forms. Reniform hematite is a mass of kidney-shaped round balls. Specular hematite is made of tiny black flakes, like mica schist. Hematite is the mineral that makes rocks reddish. It is one of the most common minerals on earth.

Rutile is the oxide of the metal titanium. Titanium, like molybdenum, is a metal used in making special kinds of very hard steel. Rutile is usually red, but the color is very dark and big crystals may look black. Sometimes rutile forms needles. These needles may be trapped inside other minerals. Rutile in quartz is usually a golden yellow color.

31

CARBONATES

The carbonates are a group of beautiful and very common minerals. They all contain metal atoms and groups of three oxygen atoms that make a tiny triangle around an atom of carbon.

Aragonite, like calcite, is made of calcium carbonate. Aragonite crystals are different from calcite crystals and are not rhomb shaped. Aragonite is made from sea water by oysters to cover the inside of their shells. This is called mother-of-pearl. Oysters also make aragonite to cover bits of sand that get inside their shells. The layers of aragonite build up around the sand and are known as pearls.

Rhodochrosite is manganese carbonate. It is always a rose-red or pink color and often forms beautiful crystals. This is one of the most popular minerals among collectors.

Azurite and malachite are two of the most beautiful and desired carbonate minerals. Both are copper carbonates and are found almost everywhere copper is mined. Azurite is a lovely dark blue color, and malachite is green. Both minerals can form in layers like sedimentary rocks, or in nodules. Sometimes they are mixed together. Azurite may form large and perfect crystals, but malachite almost never forms crystals.

Calcite is the most common carbonate. It makes up the rock limestone. It is also the mineral produced from sea water by thousands of different marine animals to make shells. Calcite is found in hundreds of crystal shapes, or habits. There are some collectors who collect only different habits of calcite crystals. Calcite is found in many different colors also.

NITRATES/BORATES

Nitrates have a nitrogen atom surrounded by three oxygen atoms. The only two important minerals in this group are niter, the nitrate of the metal potassium, and soda niter, the nitrate of sodium. Both minerals are found in dry, desert areas, because both minerals dissolve easily in water!

Colemanite is a calcium borate that forms perfect, colorless crystals. California is the most important place to find them.

There are more than 100 borate minerals, but only a few are commonly found. Almost all are colorless (or white), soft, and delicate.

Borax forms clear, perfect crystals that quickly turn white as they dry. Borax has been used for hundreds of years as a medicine and for cleaning. Borax is sold in stores, along with soap powders, for washing clothes. Borax usually forms when salt lakes dry up. Kernite is similar to borax but does not form good crystals. It is found only in the Mojave Desert in California, where there are millions of tons of kernite.

Ulexite is an unusual borate. It forms masses of long needles all packed tightly together. These have a "satiny" look when seen from the side. But if you grind and polish the ends of a mass of these fibers, you discover something amazing. The stone appears to be as clear as glass when you look down the length of the fibers! Polished pieces of ulexite are sometimes called "TV stone" because looking at a polished end is like looking at a TV screen.

SULFATES & CHROMATES

Barite is the most common sulfate mineral. It is a sulfate of the element barium. The name barite comes from the Greek word "barys," which means "heavy." Barite is so heavy that if you make a fine powder out of it and mix it with water, rock chips will float in the "mud." This special mud is used in drilling oil wells. The mud is pumped down the drill pipe to wash up pieces of rock at the bottom. Barite forms in a wide variety of crystal shapes and colors. Some crystals are very large.

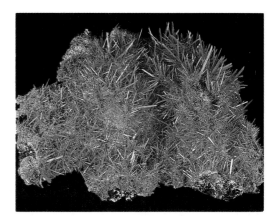

Crocoite is the only chromate mineral that is important to collectors. It is the chromate of lead. This is a wonderful, bright red mineral. It is very rare, and good specimens come only from one place—Dundas, Tasmania.

Gypsum is probably the most common sulfate. It is often found in caves, where it can form huge crystals. Ground-up gypsum is used to make the building material called plaster of Paris. Gypsum has a Mohs hardness of two, and can be scratched with your fingernail. The variety called selenite is clear. Another variety is called satin spar. Alabaster is solid, massive gypsum. Thick beds of gypsum are formed by evaporation of sea water.

Minerals in these groups are brightly colored and form lovely crystals that are prized by collectors.

Celestite and anglesite are the sulfates of strontium and lead. Celestite is almost always white or pale blue in color. The Malagsy Republic has a spot where perfect, sometimes clear celestite crystals are found in geodes. Anglesite is usually found together with other lead minerals, such as galena. It comes from many places in the world.

PHOSPHATES, ARSENATES, & VANADATES

Apatite is calcium phosphate. It is one of the apatite group of phosphates, which contain four minerals (apatite, pyromorphite, mimetite, vanadinite). It is the most common phosphate mineral, and it is found all over the world. Collectors can often find large crystals. The colors are usually green, yellow, or brown, but can be dark pink or dark blue. Apatite is used as a fertilizer.

Turquoise, a copper phosphate, is always blue or green and has been used as a gemstone for thousands of years.

These minerals are secondary. This means they formed when other minerals were broken apart or were altered.

Mimetite is similar to pyromorphite. Mimetite is a lead arsenate.

Vanadinite, lead vanadate, is one of the most popular of all minerals. It forms bright red groups of crystals, and they cover rock surfaces.

Erythrite, a bright purple mineral known best from Morocco, is an arsenate of the metal cobalt.

35

TUNGSTATES & MOLYBDATES

Wolframite is iron tungstate, and forms black, shiny, and very perfect crystals. Tungsten, like molybdenum, is a very important metal that is used to make steel harder.

Scheelite is calcium tungstate, a lovely yellow or colorless mineral that forms crystals up to several inches across.

The best known mineral in this group is one of the minerals that every collector wants to own: wulfenite.

Wulfenite is lead molybdate, and forms perfect crystals that look like square wafers. These come in several colors: yellow, brown, orange, and red. Wulfenite crystals are very pretty and can be large. Wulfenite is also a common mineral in lead mines. The most famous source is the Red Cloud Mine in Arizona.

SILICATES

Single Tetrahedra

Topaz is a popular mineral with collectors. It is found as perfect crystals in locations all over the world. The biggest crystals can weigh 100 pounds and still have perfect shapes. Topaz can be colorless, yellow, blue, pink, or orange.

Olivine is a group of minerals that melt at a very high temperature. These minerals are among the first to form crystals when magma starts to cool deep within the earth. The gemstone cut from olivine is called peridot.

All silicates are made of metal elements and a silicon tetrahedron. This is an atom of the element silicon surrounded by four oxygen atoms. The oxygen atoms are arranged in a tetrahedron.

Garnets are found in many rocks in all parts of the world. The garnet family includes a dozen minerals. Six of them are well known: pyrope, almandine, spessartine, uvarovite, grossular, and andradite. All the garnets form beautiful crystals. Most garnets are either red, orange, or brown. Some come in many different colors, including shades of yellow, green, purple, and red. Garnets are important gemstones.

Two Tetrahedra

Epidote is a common mineral, usually brown or green. The epidote group also includes other minerals. One of them, zoisite, is found in Africa as large, clear blue crystals. These can be turned into an even darker blue by heating them. Cut gemstones made from these crystals are called tanzanite.

37

SILICATES

Silicates make up about half of the earth's crust. About one quarter of all known minerals are silicates.

Rings of Tetrahedra

Beryl is one of the best known of all minerals. It is found all over the world, usually in pegmatites. It can form huge crystals, some of them weighing many tons. These giants are opaque—you cannot see into them. Beryl does form completely clear crystals in all colors, and some of these can still be large. Beryl is often cut and polished as a gemstone, and each color has a different gem name. The most popular beryl colors are blue, green, pink, and yellow.

Chains of Tetrahedra

Spodumene is a silicate of the element lithium. It is a member of the pyroxene family. It can form giant crystals 40 feet long, but these are very rare and are opaque. Clear crystals up to three feet long have been found in Brazil and Afghanistan. The color can be pink, green, or yellow. Spodumene is sometimes cut and polished as a gemstone.

Tourmaline is another ring silicate that is found in pegmatites all over the world. Tourmaline comes in many colors—probably more than any other mineral. Some tourmaline crystals can be several feet long. Many of these have two or more colors—they change color along their length. Watermelon tourmaline is pink on the inside and green on the outside. Tourmaline is a very popular gemstone.

Hornblende is one of the most common members of the amphibole family. Crystals are dark green or black. Tremolite is a white amphibole. It forms long, thin crystals that look like hairs. These can grow together to make a solid mass—it looks a little like the matted hair of a wet dog!

Sheets of Tetrahedra

Talc, a very soft mineral, almost never forms crystals. Talc is familiar to everyone—mothers use talcum powder on babies to keep them dry!

Corner-Linked Tetrahedra

Feldspar is the name of a large group of minerals that are present in almost all igneous rocks. The feldspars are divided into two groups based on chemistry. These are called potassium feldspars and plagioclase feldspars. The important potassium feldspars are called orthoclase and microcline. A pretty blue type of microcline is known as amazonite. The plagioclase

group includes albite, oligoclase, andesine, labradorite, bytownite, and anorthite.

Most of the earth's crust is made of corner-linked tetrahedra minerals.

Biotite is a member of the mica group, which is a family of related minerals that all have perfect cleavage. Sheets that have been split off these minerals can be bent quite a bit without breaking.

Quartz is one of the most common minerals on earth. Quartz is found in many kinds of rocks. When these rocks are weathered, the quartz grains may wind up as desert, river, or beach sand. Quartz crystals come in different colors and can be cut as gemstones.

PRECIOUS METALS & GEMS

are not only beautiful to look at, but some people believe they hold almost magical powers. In older times, people thought certain mineral crystals helped people born in certain months. That is why we now have birthstones.

For centuries, poets and songwriters have compared beautiful women to precious metals and gems. Men give women diamond rings to tell them they want to marry them. The value of gold, silver, diamonds, and emeralds is not just how much they cost.

Not all precious crystal minerals look like the stones in jewelry stores. Crystals are cut and polished to bring out the sparkle and shine. Valuable metals are often mixed with other metal to make them harder. This is the case with gold. Pure gold is very soft and would bend easily if it were made into a ring.

PRECIOUS METALS

Copper, silver, and gold (below) often form interesting shapes.

Most of the known minerals are chemical compounds. They contain different kinds of atoms arranged in regular patterns. But some minerals are elements. The metals that are found by themselves are called native metals, and there are only a few.

Copper is an important metal, but it is not expensive. Other native metals are gold, silver, and platinum. These are quite very valuable. For centuries, gold and silver have been thought of as treasure. These metals have been symbols of wealth since the beginning of history.

Gold and silver form natural crystals that are very beautiful. Gold crystals are usually found in "veins," thin layers of white quartz that have filled in cracks in certain rocks. Platinum seldom forms crystals. But all three metals are found as lumps called "nuggets." Some of these nuggets are very large. The "Welcome Stranger" gold nugget, found in Australia in 1869, weighed more than 150 pounds. An even bigger silver nugget was found in Mexico around 1820.

GEMS

Gems are valuable. Some gems, like pearls and amber, are made by living things. Most gems are minerals, but not all minerals are gems! Gems are usually (but not always) hard, rare, and pretty. Not everyone agrees about what "pretty" looks like. So people often have different ideas about what minerals should be called gems.

Minerals, as we have seen, come in many colors. A single mineral, like tourmaline, may be found in dozens of different colors. Different colors of a single mineral are called varieties.

Corundum, an oxide mineral, is found in dozens of colors. Gemstones cut out of all colors of corundum, except red, are called sapphire. Red corundum has its own special name: ruby.

Beryl is also found in many colors. Dark green beryl is called emerald. Pink beryl is morganite. The blue or blue-green variety of beryl is called aquamarine. Colorless (pure) beryl is called goshenite. Yellow beryl is called heliodor or golden beryl.

Garnets are used as gems, especially almandine, spessartine, rhodolite, and grossular. The color varieties of grossular are some of the loveliest of all.

Gemstones are made by grinding minerals to a certain shape and then polishing them. Faceted stones are polished with small flat surfaces called facets. These facets make the gemstone sparkle.

Diamond is one of the most valuable gemstones. Colorless diamonds are very rare.

A natural crystal looks much different when it is polished and cut.

It is truly amazing that the earth can produce such beautiful and interesting objects as mineral crystals!

GLOSSARY

Atom (AT-uhm): The smallest bit of material that can be called an element. Atoms can exist alone or may combine with other atoms to form molecules.

Chemical sedimentary rock (KEM-i-kuhl sed-uh-MENT-uh-ree RAHK): Atoms and molecules floating in sea water clump together to form tiny crystals of minerals. These tiny crystals may get large enough to sink to the bottom and form thick layers that eventually become rock.

Cleavage (KLEE-vij): A mineral property that describes the way a crystal breaks along certain planes.

Compound (KAHM-paund): A substance made of two or more different elements.

Crystal (KRIS-tuhl): A solid made of atoms and molecules joined together in rows and layers that create a smooth pattern.

Element (EL-uh-muhnt): A substance made of only one kind of atom.

Erosion (i-RO-zhuhn): The breaking apart of rocks when exposed to rain, wind, and ice.

Extrusive rocks (ik-STROO-siv RAHKZ): Rocks that are formed when magma cools on the earth's surface.

Fossil (FAHS-uhl): The remains or traces of an animal or plant left in rock.

Geologist (jee-AYL-uh-juhst): A scientist who studies geology.

Geology (jee-AYL-uh-jee): The science that deals with the earth, its rocks, and the changes taking place now and in the past.

Habit (HAB-uht): The shape made by combining groups of crystal surfaces. Minerals can have many different habits even though they are made of the same atoms and molecules.

Igneous rock (IG-nee-uhs RAHK): Rocks that are made of magma that has cooled.

Impurity (im-PYUHR-uht-ee): An atom in a crystal that does not normally belong in the crystal structure.

Intrusive rocks (in-TROO-siv RAHKZ): Rocks that are formed when magma cools inside the earth.

Lava (LAHV-uh): The fluid magma that flows out of a volcano.

Magma (MAG-muh): The fluid or liquid rock that has not cooled to form solid rock.

Mechanical sedimentary rock (mi-KAN-i-kuhl sed-uh-MENT-uh-ree RAHK): Pieces of weathered rock that are cemented or pressed together in a lake, stream bed, or ocean.

Metamorphic rock (met-uh-MAHR-fik RAHK): The heat and pressure within the earth melts and squeezes older rocks, which then take a new form.

Mineral (MIN-uh-ruhl): A naturally occurring element or compound that forms crystals. Every mineral has a unique combination made of certain atoms and a particular crystal structure.

Mohs (MOZ) **Hardness Scale:** Arranges minerals according to how easily they scratch each other.

Molecule (MAHL-i-kyool): A clump made of two or more atoms. It is the smallest possible piece of a compound.

Ore (OR): A mineral that is mined for a part of its chemical make-up, such as the metals silver or copper.

Rock (RAHK): Rocks are made of one or several minerals. Silicates are the main rock-building minerals.

Stalactite (stuh-LAK-tyt): When water that contains dissolved minerals evaporates, leaving minerals behind. It is a cave formation that grows down from the ceiling that may look like an icicle.

Stalagmite (stuh-LAG-myt): Formed in the same way as a stalactite, but it is a hill-shaped cave formation.

Volcano (vahl-KAY-no): A hill or mountain made of lava. If still active, a volcano will erupt and send lava flowing or shooting out of its center.

Weathering (WETH-uhr-ing): The breaking down of rocks by rain, ice, wind, and acids made by tiny plants.